At That
Moment

DAWN MARIE NAPPI, PHD.

WESTBOW
PRESS®
A DIVISION OF THOMAS NELSON
& ZONDERVAN

Cover Art by Bernadette DeNyse

A portion of the proceeds from the sale of this book
will be donated to MADD, Long Island

WestBow Press books may be ordered through booksellers or by contacting:

WestBow Press
A Division of Thomas Nelson & Zondervan
1663 Liberty Drive
Bloomington, IN 47403
www.westbowpress.com
1 (866) 928-1240

ISBN: 978-1-5127-3547-5 (sc)
ISBN: 978-1-5127-3549-9 (hc)
ISBN: 978-1-5127-3548-2 (e)

Library of Congress Control Number: 2016904800

Print information available on the last page.

WestBow Press rev. date: 4/14/2016

In Loving Memory of

Angelica Perna Nappi

October 23, 1993–February 22, 2008

The day that I was born back in 1993,
My parents took one look, God's angel they did see.
I was their "Angelica," a piece of heaven here on Earth,
I touched the lives of many all across the earth.
My fourteen years with you have been nothing but the best,
But an angel sent from God is not idle; doesn't rest.
So I'm off to be united with my Father up above,
Upon the impact with the car, I was surrounded by His love.
Do not grieve for me, my loved ones;
I'm at peace, you soon shall see,
I wish that I could take you straight to heaven here with me.
So carry on with your life, and find comfort in His love,
I am always there in spirit, watching from above.

To my angel, Angelica, whose life on Earth was a brief fourteen years. I truly believe you were an angel in disguise, an answer to Mommy's heartfelt prayer. You were sent here from heaven to do a quick work. Undoubtedly, the lives you touched are many, both in your life and in your legacy. I am ever so grateful to God for granting me the privilege and honor to mother you for those years. The memories I have are treasured in my heart. Until the day that I reunite with you in paradise, please know that I carry you in my heart. Until we meet again, my precious girl.

To my daughter Nicolette, I love you and am so proud of the beautiful woman you have become. You have endured much pain at a tender, young age, but God has graced you with His strength. Daddy and I have always told you that God spared your life that day for a reason. You have a mighty work to do for His kingdom. Angelica is proud of you. I imagine her smiling that radiant smile of hers in gratitude for all that you do in her memory. Together we will share our story of hope.

To my son Joseph, I love you to the moon and back. I know that you never understood or accepted the death of your sister. You chose to close out that chapter of your life. I pray that the healing power of God touches you and that you find your way back to Him. Remember, God doesn't cause evil or heartache.

We live in a fallen world. God never left us during that low point in our lives. He was with us in the valley, and we will be with Him on the mountaintop. Continue to press on toward the mark of the high calling in Christ Jesus. Never, ever lose hope.

To my son Avellino, I believe that your sissy in heaven had a part in sending you here to Earth. You have blessed our family and restored so much joy back to our home. You made us laugh when we never thought we could again. We see glimpses of Angelica in your expressions and are reminded that Angelica is here with us in spirit. Thank you for being the sweet, lovable boy that you are.

To my husband, Joseph, my love for you continues to grow stronger each day. We are proof of God's faithfulness in the darkest hour. Prayer has pulled us through and kept us strong when we thought all hope was lost. Together we have weathered the storms, the worst being the death of our child. I am in awe at how your faith has matured and how you have grown spiritually. When I was weak, you were strong, and somehow we always seemed to balance each other out. We learned that tragedy can tear apart, but it can also restore. I am thankful to God for making beautiful things come from our devastating circumstances.

To my mom and dad, you have both recently gone home to be with the Lord. I never understood your worry and concern until I became a parent myself. Thank you for giving me the best of everything in my formative years. Your love and support have carried me through and served as an example for me. The Bible says that whoever builds his life on a spiritual foundation is "like a man which built a house, and digged deep, and laid the foundation on a rock: and when the flood arose, the stream beat vehemently upon that house, and could not shake it: for it was founded upon a rock" (Luke 6:47–48). Thank you for laying the spiritual groundwork in my life. The seeds you have sown have taken root and allowed me to remain standing in the face of adversity. Without them I never would have made it.

To my sisters, Kim, Lynn, and Gwenn, I am so grateful for you all. There is nothing better than sisterly love. Thank you for always being there for me and my family. No matter which direction life takes us, you will be close to my heart. I love you all.

To my friends and colleagues, thank you for your love and support. You have stood by my side and have always been there to lend an ear or offer a shoulder to cry on. Please know how much I appreciate you today and always.

To my brother in law, Anthony, and sister-in law, Andrea, thank you for never leaving my side. Your strength helped carry Joe and me through the darkest time of our life.

To mom and dad Nappi, God blessed me with a second pair of parents. Please know how much I love and appreciate you for all that you do.

To the man responsible for Angelica's death, I forgive you. Thank you for showing me the true meaning of mercy. Please know that I pray for you each and every day, and I know that Angelica is too. I pray that Angelica's death is your catalyst for change.

To all those suffering at the hands of addiction, there is hope for you. It lies in the strength that only Jesus Christ Himself can give. You don't have to live under the stronghold of your addiction anymore. Christ died so that you, yes, *you*, can have life more abundantly. Give Him a try. I promise that you won't be disappointed.

To my Lord and Savior, Jesus Christ, thank you for shedding your precious blood on the cross for *me*. I have failed many times to live in a manner that is worthy of your calling. Thank you for your mercy and grace when I failed to witness for you in my thoughts, words, and deeds. Nothing that I do in this lifetime could ever repay you for what you have done. It is my hope that this book will encourage others to seek your face in the midst of their storm. All glory, honor, and praise belongs to you.

I still hear your voice, I still feel your touch

And when I close my eyes, I can see your smile

Though you're gone away to a better place

I can't wait to be with you

After while.

—Deitrick Haddon

Foreword

"AT THAT MOMENT" is the loving work of Dawn Nappi PhD, whom I have known since her daughter Angelica's tragic death.

Dr. Nappi's book is must reading for anyone who drives, has children, and is disappointed by the way our justice system treats behind the wheel "killers".

Since losing her daughter Angelica, Dr. Nappi has dedicated herself to tirelessly working to toughen penalties in our Vehicle & Traffic code, and hopefully to pass what some lawmakers have coined "Angelica's Law". Until now, a New York state driver who is suspended or revoked and gets behind the wheel and injures or kills due to their negligence, only faces a misdemeanor, a slap on the wrist. Angelica's Law would raise those penalties to felony status, and for flagrant offenders of driving suspended or revoked, it would mean up to 4 years in prison.

I urge you to join Dr. Nappi's fight to make our highways safer for all.

-Drew Scott, News 12 Long Island

Blessed be God, even the Father of our Lord Jesus Christ, the Father of mercies, and the God of all comfort; Who comforteth us in all our tribulation, that we may be able to comfort them which are in any trouble, by the comfort wherewith we ourselves are comforted of God. (2 Corinthians 1:3–4)

Preface

My dear sisters and brothers in Christ,

All praise, glory, and honor be to our Lord and Savior, Jesus Christ. It is Jesus himself who has kept me through the darkest moments of my life. It is Jesus who has carried me, kept me, and allowed me to witness to you through the words of this book. I pray that the power of the Holy Spirit will touch you in your innermost being as I share with you my personal Calvary.

It is written that we "overcome by one another's testimonies." It is my utmost and heartfelt desire that as you read and reflect on this personal journey of tragedy and restoration that you are renewed in your body, mind, soul, and spirit. Jehovah Rapha is indeed our healer, and he is faithful. Jehovah Shalom is able to provide peace in the midst of life's most devastating storms. It was at that moment of complete brokenness that I experienced the healing power of God. May you also come to know just how real and awesome our God really is. Reach out and touch the hem of his garment. I guarantee that you will be forever changed.

Chapter 1

Lo, children are an heritage of the LORD: and the fruit of the womb is his reward. (Psalm 127:3)

Every weeknight I attended the 5:00 Mass. I begged God from the bottom of my heart to allow me to conceive immediately. I had heard many stories of couples who had tried for years to become pregnant, and I was petrified that would happen to me and further delay my lifelong dream of being a mommy. I knew Joey and I would begin trying just as soon as we had exchanged our vows. As eager as I was to pursue my teaching career, motherhood was second to none. I had wanted to have a baby since I was a young girl. Being the youngest of four, I never had the chance to nurture a sibling, and I longed to put my motherly instincts to work in rearing a child of my own.

> I am the woman who stood by you here praying to the Lord. For this child I prayed, and the Lord has granted me my petitions which I asked of Him. (1 Samuel 1:26–27)

Within the first month of trying to conceive, that wonderful pink line miraculously appeared on the EPT stick. Oh, the joy in seeing that line gradually appear in the test-area window! My eyes were glued as I waited impatiently to see whether God had honored my prayer this quickly. There it was, faint, but still apparent and convincing. *I was* pregnant*! I was going to have a baby! We were going to be parents!* It was a dream. A wonderful, wonderful dream that I couldn't believe I was having. I quickly announced the news to my husband of only one month.

"Jo-eeeeeeeyyyyyyyyyyyyy!" I screamed. *"We're pregnant!"*

"No way!" he replied. "Are you sure you did it right? You can't be!"

Without further ado, we headed off to the doctor, took another test to confirm, and indeed, we were pregnant. We were going to have a honeymoon baby. God had surely answered my prayer.

Chapter 2

The effectual fervent prayer of the righteous availeth much. (James 5:6)

I could have screamed from the mountaintops. I wanted the whole world to know that I was going to have a baby. I immediately took on that pregnancy glow and sported maternity clothes even before the first noticeable pregnancy bump. Life couldn't have been better. I was going to be a mother and soon would be a part of the diaper-changing, baby-burping, and round-the-clock nursing world.

Nine months couldn't come soon enough. I journaled to Baby Nappi every day, thanking him or her for the blessing of motherhood. I felt like the luckiest person alive. I couldn't wait to give birth to my long-awaited child.

After what seemed like an eternity, Angelica Perna Nappi made her grand entrance into the world. She arrived on her actual due date, Saturday, October 23, 1993, at 9:16 a.m. After three long days of labor and travail, I came face-to-face with our six-pound, fourteen-ounce, twenty-and-a-half-inch blessing from the Lord. The windows of heaven had opened that day, and Joey and I were on top of the world.

> Her children arise up, and call her blessed; her husband also, and he praiseth her. (Proverbs 31:28)

Motherhood was all that I had hoped and dreamed and more. I cherished motherhood so much that Angelica was soon blessed with a sister, Nicolette, and a brother, Joseph. Angelica and Nicolette were like twins, being only sixteen months apart. Joseph arrived nineteen months after Nicolette, so it wouldn't be amiss to say it was like mothering triplets at times.

I loved being a mommy. It was exhausting but so completely satisfying. I remember staring at my children as they slept, in awe at how they could make life so complete. I admit I was completely smitten.

Angelica never wanted to leave my side. Everywhere I went, she would follow. Even as a young child of nine or ten, she would rather spend time with me than go off with a friend.

She would call me after school on my phone and inquire about my whereabouts. She insisted that I wait for her so she could "come too." It was almost as if she were maximizing the time we had left together.

Raising our kids provided us with many wonderful memories. Some of our fondest were vacationing at Wildwood each summer and staying at the Aqua Beach Resort. Being a lover of high tea, I soon exposed the kids to this English ritual, and we began frequenting teahouses in different states. It became our tradition for the kids and me to have a holiday tea each December at Teaberry's in Flemington. This soon become Angelica's favorite tearoom and the location for our annual Christmas card photo.

Train up a child in the way he should go, and when he is old he will not depart from it. (Proverbs 22:6)

The years went by, and the kids practically grew beneath our noses, or so it seemed. It wasn't long before Angelica started her freshman year at Sachem North High School, and Nicolette and Joseph were attending Seneca Middle School. I had resumed my teaching career when Joseph turned two and continued on to pursue my master's and PhD. Joey was still working long hours for UPS, but besides the daily demands of life, we were a normal family.

Despite the typical sibling quarreling, Angelica, Nicolette, and Joseph loved each other and did everything together. I considered them the Three Musketeers. One thing I insisted on was that we attend church regularly. Eventually, the girls became part of the praise dance ministry. The very first and last dance they performed together was to "After While" by Deitrick Haddon. I later realized the significance of the lyrics and how later on they would become a source of comfort.

Chapter 3

Blessed are they that mourn, for they shall be comforted. (Matthew 5:4)

O ver the February 2008 winter break, my pastor's nineteen-year-old daughter hosted a much-awaited sleepover. She invited Angelica and Nicolette and another girl from the church. They had planned on seeing a movie the following day and then heading to the mall in the afternoon to do some shopping. I remember dropping the girls off at the house that night. It was around 6:00 p.m., and there was a light drizzle. Nicolette anxiously said good night and exited the car.

Angelica was sitting up front in the passenger seat. I kept asking her if she really wanted to spend the night because she was battling a sinus infection. She assured me that she did.

I kissed her good night, we exchanged I love yous, and she headed out, pillow in hand.

As I watched her walk to the door, I remember thinking, *What if I never see her again?* I honestly don't know why that thought entered my mind, but I dismissed it and somberly drove back home.

The next morning, I began my day with my usual routine of having coffee in my favorite rocking chair. This was my quiet time with the Lord when I could pray, reflect, and meditate before beginning the tasks of the day. As I was pondering how the girls' sleepover went—I had not heard from either of them since the night before—I thought about their plans to drive to the movies later that day. It was then that I felt a strong desire to go in my bedroom, get on my knees, and pray for the kids' safety in the car.

I took it as nothing more than an overprotective mother simply worrying about her kids being passengers in someone else's car. Nevertheless, I went into my bedroom, knelt down, and prayed for traveling mercies. It wasn't until approximately an hour and a half later that I understood why.

Chapter 4

For the thing I greatly feared has come upon me, and what I dreaded has happened to me. (Job 3:25)

I love vacations. After all, what teacher doesn't? It was Tuesday, February 19, and school was recessed for winter break. The weather was crisp but sunny. I was excited to have lunch at Panera Bread with my colleague John and his mother, who also worked in our district. My son, Joseph, and his friend had decided to come too.

We had just finished eating our lunch and were discussing our dessert options when my cell phone rang. I answered it, but the call dropped. I looked at the caller ID and saw that Nicolette had called. I figured she was just touching base and waited for her to call back.

Seconds later, she called again. I answered, but we lost the connection. I excused myself from the table to go outside in hopes of getting a better signal.

My phone rang again. It was Nicolette. She was screaming, "Mommy, Mommy, Angelica's heart rate is really low, and they are rushing her to the hospital!"

As I was trying to process what Nicolette was saying, I thought that maybe Angelica hadn't eaten and her blood sugar had gotten too low, so they were taking her to the hospital as a precaution.

The next thing I knew, I heard an unfamiliar male voice speaking into the phone. The voice urged me to get to the hospital as soon as possible because my daughter was critical. I screamed, *"What do you mean? They were in an accident?"* I then realized that an ambulance EMT had taken the phone from Nicolette.

I dropped to my knees in the parking lot of Panera Bread and screamed, "No! No! No! No!" I refused to believe what I was hearing. This couldn't be happening! I remembered my prayer from an hour and a half earlier. At that moment, while screaming *no* from the depth of my soul, I knew Angelica was going to die.

Chapter 5

And God is able to make all grace abound toward you; that ye, always having all sufficiency in all things, may abound to every good work. (2 Corinthians 9:8)

God is so good. John was with me that day because God knew I would be in no condition to drive. When I look back at it now, he had everything in place for the moment of crisis. Joseph was with me too, just where he needed to be.

John's NASCAR talents came into play that day. We made it to the hospital with record-breaking speed. I remember crying out to God, "My baby can't die! My baby can't die!" I called my husband to inform him of the accident and told him that Angelica was critical. Nicolette had already contacted him as well as other family members, who were already en route

11

to the hospital. Joey was unaware of the severity of Angelica's condition. He believed it was only a precautionary measure rather than a life-or-death situation. He immediately returned his truck to the UPS base and left to meet me at the hospital.

When we arrived at the hospital, Angelica had just been rushed into CAT scan. My sister-in-law, Andrea, had already arrived, and she informed me that Nicolette was on a gurney in the hallway. She was fine other than being totally shaken up.

Someone ushered me into a family room to wait until we heard about Angelica's condition. I knew that the family room was the place they sent you when the situation was bleak. It was the gathering place so the entire family could be together when they received the devastating news. The family room was not a good place to be.

> Hear my prayer, O Lord, and give ear to my cry. Do not be silent at my tears ... (Psalm 39:12)

While waiting for my husband to arrive, my friends from church and I found a nearby bathroom and began praying out loud to the Lord. Praying from the depths of my soul, I begged God to spare the life of my daughter. I remembered the story of Job, how he had lost several of his children at once. I thanked God for sparing the life of my other daughter,

Nicolette. I recalled the prayer that I had said that morning and believed that God had directly intervened from his throne. I later learned that if the car my daughters were driving in had been going just a bit slower, the jeep that crashed into them would have made direct contact with the fuel tank, most likely causing an explosion.

> Yea, though I walk through the valley of the shadow of death, I will fear no evil; for thou art with me; thy rod and thy staff they comfort me. (Psalm 23:4)

It wasn't long before Joey arrived. I saw the look of despair on his face as he barreled down the corridor, waiting to receive news on his daughters. A neurosurgeon came out and informed us that Angelica's brain was so severely swollen that they had to do immediate surgery to remove a section of her skull. Joey said, "Whatever you need to do to save my baby, do it."

By this time, family members from all of the crash victims were arriving at the hospital. I was still unclear as to what exactly had taken place and was curious to find out the facts. It turned out that the girls were involved in a three-car crash and were struck directly in the intersection of 101 and Woodside Avenue. Apparently, a man ran through a red light and hit the car the girls were riding in. The impact was directly on

Angelica's side. She was sitting directly behind Rachel, our pastor's daughter, who was the driver. Nicolette was sitting in the passenger seat. Apparently, Nicolette and Angelica had switched seats right before they left the house. Angelica chose the window seat because she didn't want Brittany, my pastor's youngest daughter, to sit there because it was "not as safe." Angelica was like a mother hen, always looking out for the well-being of others. Brittany, therefore, ended up sitting to Angelica's right. Tanisha, our pastor's other daughter, was next to Brittany, and Maggie, Angelica's best friend, was behind the front-seat passenger, Nicolette.

Nicolette recalled the car spinning around several times before coming to a tumultuous stop. She turned around and saw Angelica slumped over in the back seat of the car. She called her name several times, but Angelica remained unresponsive. The driver-side airbag had deployed, and Rachel was bleeding from her mouth. Brittany was in and out of consciousness, and the other girls were in a state of shock.

The car that ran the red light plowed into another vehicle, seriously injuring the driver. Several of the passengers were air lifted to the hospital.

Life for me had become painfully ironic. Two weeks prior to the crash, I had taken Angelica to the pediatrician for her physical. The pediatrician asked her if she wore her seatbelt when she was in the car. Angelica responded with an emphatic yes but asked why it was necessary to wear a seatbelt if you were sitting in the backseat of the car. The pediatrician responded with a story about a sixteen-year-old patient who sat in the backseat of the car and neglected to wear her seatbelt. Unfortunately, she got into an accident and was thrown through the windshield of the car. Angelica relayed that story while she buckled up that day, informing the girls that she did not want to die.

Chapter 6

My flesh and my heart faileth, but God is the strength of my heart, and my portion forever. (Psalm 73:26)

hortly after they took Angelica into the OR, the head surgeon came out and summoned us into his office, where he matter-of-factly stated that Angelica was brain dead. He spoke these words in the same tone as if he were ordering a Big Mac at the drive thru.

Angelica is brain dead. Brain DEAD. BRAIN dead. BRAIN DEAD. Brain death, as described by Web MD, is the complete and irreversible loss of brain function, including involuntary activity necessary to sustain life. *Complete. Irreversible. Permanent. As in there is no turning back.* I couldn't process what he had just said. "NO! NO! NO!" I screamed. I flailed my arms in disbelief, sending my cup of water airborne.

Joey, his brother Anthony (Angelica's godfather), my oldest sister, Kim, and her husband, Tony, my pastor, the surgeon, and I were piled into a tiny office somewhere away from the family room. This room was worse than the family room. This was the room that revealed the fate of my baby. The brain-dead room. When I was in the family room, my baby was at least still alive and not brain dead. It was safer in that room. I still had hope in that room. This room was a nightmare room. I was having a nightmare, and I couldn't wake myself up. I refused to believe that my vibrant, fourteen-year-old daughter was brain dead. Incapable of moving, thinking, dancing, smiling.

NOOOOOOOOOOOOOOOOOOOOOOOOOOOOOOOOO OOOOOOOOOOOOOOOOOOOOOOOOOOOOOOOOOO OOOOOOOOOOOOOOOOOOOOOOOOO! I grabbed at my hair, hoping to pull it out by the roots. I needed the pain, that electrifying sensation of disbelief, to leave my body. If it wasn't going to leave on its own, I would yank it out by pulling out my hair. In the middle of my rage, I screamed at the doctor, "My baby is *not* brain dead! I refuse to accept this! God is going to help her!" I frantically looked around the nightmare room, wondering why nobody was joining my plea in Angelica's defense. Pastor was sobbing heart-wrenching tears. I remember stroking his back, telling him that Angelica would be all right. God was God, right? He was still in the miracle-working business, wasn't he? He wouldn't let Angelica die. She was only fourteen. She loved God, and God loved her. She danced for him, so how could this be happening?

My entire world came crashing down. I felt like I, too, had died. Every fiber of my being froze. I felt dead physically, emotionally, and mentally. I imagined Calvary and how Jesus must have felt, knowing that there was no escaping the fate that awaited him. Just like there was no escaping this fate that awaited the Nappi family. A fate that involved living life without Angelica.

Chapter 7

Blessed are the pure in heart, for they shall see God. (Matthew 5:8)

The Sunday before the crash, Angelica had stayed behind to talk with the pastor after church. I grew impatient as I waited for her to come out and get in the car. After a good forty-five minutes, she came strolling out with a satisfied look on her face. It wasn't until Pastor delivered his speech that I learned of the nature of their conversation. He explained that Angelica wanted God to be happy with her, and she wanted reassurance that she was doing his will. To this day, I wonder if part of her knew she would be going home to be with the Lord. What made her ask that question on that particular Sunday?

The Lord is near to those who have a broken heart. (Psalm 34:18)

The time had come, and we were finally able to see Angelica. Her room was located at the far end of the hallway. Joey and his sister started ahead, and I proceeded behind them. I locked arms with my brother-in-law in hopes that if my legs gave way he would hold me up. But my legs wouldn't move. I made a conscious effort to put one foot in front of the other, but it felt as though lead weights were holding me down. My brother-in-law suggested that he go in before me, but I adamantly insisted that I go too. But I was so gripped with fear and prayed that I wouldn't collapse at the first sight of my daughter.

We walked in, uncertain as to what we might see. Fear and shock strangled our vocal chords. Not a sound could be heard except the beeping of monitors and the artificial breathing of the life support. There was Angelica, lying lifeless in the bed. Shards of glass were embedded in the left side of her beautiful, porcelain-skinned face. A cervical collar was around her neck. Her right eyelid formed a baseball-sized lump, causing her eyes to be merely opened slits. Her head was bandaged like a mummy. It appeared as though her beautiful hair was wrapped turban-style in a towel, much like after taking a shower. I later learned that it was her brain and the profuse swelling that I saw. Her hair had been cut and her skull removed to allow the brain the necessary room to swell without constraint. The blood-stained bandages reminded me of an episode of *ER,* except this was reality in my face. Intracranial tubes were draining brain fluids and IVs penetrated my daughter's tiny arms.

I pulled the blanket back and saw Angelica's toes, freshly painted neon orange. She looked so helpless, and as her mother, I was helpless too. Throughout the fourteen years of caregiving, I never felt as helpless as I did that day standing alongside her bed.

Joey found his voice and called, "Bums, it's Daddy. Can you hear me?" Angelica continued to lay there, unresponsive. Joey, Anthony, and I exchanged glances, trying to read one another's expressions. I remember thinking that I would never again hear my daughter speak to or answer me ever again.

It was surreal that this was actually happening and wasn't a nightmare. How could our life be so dramatically changed within a second? The reality was beginning to set in. Angelica would never be coming home, walking, talking, laughing, smiling, or anything *ever.* She was brain dead, and I would live to bury my child.

Chapter 8

Rejoice with them that do rejoice, and weep with them that weep. (Romans 12:15)

The hospital was packed. Visitors streamed in steadily, offering support and prayers for our family. The nursing staff was more than obliging, allowing anyone with our permission to visit Angelica.

It was brought to our attention that the man responsible for the crash was located across the hall in police custody. Apparently, the police alleged that he was driving under the influence of drugs, and they were awaiting the results from toxicology. The news media had continuous widespread coverage, reporting ten injuries and one critical (Angelica). The road was closed for several hours, as a crime scene investigation was underway.

Pastor's daughter, Brittany, was listed in critical condition. Her skull had been fractured from the impact of Angelica's head hitting hers. The other girls sustained injuries that thankfully were not life threatening.

We later learned that the man responsible for the crash was an unlicensed driver with eleven previous suspensions. The toxicology report showed trace amounts of heroin in his system, but it wouldn't be enough to convict him. The man who killed our daughter would get off on minimal charges while our lives were shattered into a million pieces.

Chapter 9

Come unto me, all ye that labour and are heavy laden, and I will give you rest. (Matthew 11:28)

Our entire family took shifts staying at Angelica's bedside around the clock. The hospital arranged a room for family members to sleep, yet remain close by.

A close friend of mine offered to drive me home late one night so I could take care of our dogs, shower, and change. I walked into my house and, as if on autopilot, I went upstairs and stood in the doorway of Angelica's room. My eyes scanned every inch of it. Everything was in its proper place, just the way she had left it. Her bed had been neatly made, awaiting the next time she would sleep in it. Never again would she be sleeping in that bed. Her leopard-themed room would never again be occupied by the girl who took such pride in its ensemble. Her school calendar hung on the wall above her desk, days proudly crossed off, marking the present-day vacation. It was more like she was counting down the days to her death.

I opened her ceramic leopard trinket dish and found a pack of Bubblicious gum neatly tucked away. There were memories of her everywhere. That was all that I had left now. Memories. Then I saw the two brass giraffes I had bought for her sitting on her shelf. One was the mommy and the other was the baby. I told Angelica that when she looked at these giraffes, she would always remember the love I had for her, even when I was in heaven. I showed her how the mommy giraffe kissed the baby giraffe and left them in that position on her shelf. Angelica looked at me and said, "Mommy, don't say that. You are going to make me cry." My own words had come back to haunt me, but it was Angelica who was in heaven, and I was the one crying.

After scanning her room one more time, I went downstairs into my bedroom and sought refuge in my closet, which was my safe haven. It was my place to pray and be alone with the Lord when I needed to shut myself away from the pressures of life. I walked in, collapsed on the floor, and began crying from the depths of my soul. I felt so alone and so scared. I didn't know how I would live life without Angelica. How could I be the happy mother and wife I used to be when I was dying on the inside? I wanted to go to sleep and never wake up. Succumbing to sheer exhaustion, I fell asleep on my closet floor.

Chapter 10

The Lord gave, and the Lord has taken away; Blessed be the name of the Lord. (Job 1:21)

ngelica failed the series of tests performed to determine definitive brain death. It was now up to Joey and me to decide the day and time to remove her from life support. Joey decided that Friday at 3:00 p.m., the hour of our Lord's death, would be the time. Since Angelica loved the Lord with all her heart and soul, we agreed that this would commemorate her faith.

A few minutes before 3:00 p.m., we gathered with our immediate family. The nurses asked us to step outside the room so they could take out the breathing tube. I remember hearing the machine shut down. The mechanical breathing tube that had kept Angelica's organs functioning ceased. There was an unnatural silence in the room, soon to be broken with gut-wrenching sobs.

The nurse allowed us back in while she listened to Angelica's heart with her stethoscope. "She's gone," she said.

Gone. My baby is gone! She never went anywhere without me, and now she is gone! Gone as in for good! Gone as in I will never *see her again!* I got that surreal feeling again and felt detached from my body and its surroundings. *How did this happen? How could this happen?* I needed to get out of the room fast because I refused to allow myself to witness the life flow out of my baby's body and watch her turn blue. Her warm skin would soon become icy to the touch, and I couldn't bear it. I had seen enough. I had to leave Brookhaven Hospital, and I never wanted to look back.

Chapter 11

I will bless the Lord at all times; His praise shall continually be in my mouth. (Psalm 34:1)

The Sunday after we removed Angelica from life support, my sister Lynn and I attended service at my church. I recall the faces on the members of the congregation upon seeing us walk in. I guess they never expected me to be at service that day. I needed to praise God and give him all the glory. God was still good, despite the circumstances. How could I turn my back on the one I needed most of all? I took comfort in knowing that Angelica was safely home in his arms and that God had never left my side.

To everything there is a season, a time for every purpose under heaven: a time to be born and a time to die. (Ecclesiastes 3:1–2)

I took such pride in picking out Angelica's crib. How could I bring myself to pick out her casket? This was absurd! Parents weren't supposed to bury their kids. This went against the normal course of life. Anthony came with us to make the arrangements. My stomach had been in knots that morning, and I was resisting the urge to throw up. Part of me wanted to vomit in hopes that I could rid myself of the pain and disbelief I was feeling.

Angelica was being taken for an autopsy, and all I could think of was that someone was going to cut into her beautiful body. Incision here, incision there. My poor baby would be mutilated. The injuries from the accident were bad enough, and now she needed an autopsy! Although I was blatantly against it, (as the cause of death was quite obvious), I was told that we had no choice in the matter, as this was a crime scene investigation. I remembered the joy of seeing that pink line appear and how I wanted to scream from the mountaintop. Now that joy had turned into a sorrow so deep and pitiful. I was feeling emotions I never knew I had, feelings that I believe only tragedy reveals.

Precious in the sight of the Lord is the death of his saints. (Psalm 116:15)

The morning of Angelica's wake, I had gone to Kinko's to copy the program for her celebration of life. While I was waiting for the attendant to assist me, I received a call from the owner of Teaberry's, the teahouse I frequented with the kids. The day after the accident, I had left a message on Susan's voicemail, telling her about the horrific crash that the girls were involved in.

When I answered the phone, Susan explained to me that she had received a visit from some lady she didn't know and had never seen before. The woman admitted that she never even knew that Teaberry's existed but that she was being sent there to deliver a message to her. The woman asked Susan if she had recently been informed about an accident that had taken the life of a little girl. Susan said she stared at the woman and asked, "Who are you?" The lady then replied that she was a messenger sent to tell her that the little girl was in heaven and that she was okay. Susan made no hesitation about calling me with the news.

Chapter 12

For my thoughts are not your thoughts, neither are your ways my ways, saith the LORD. (Isaiah 55:8)

hile in the kitchen one day, I was talking aloud to God, asking him, "Why Angelica? Why her out of everyone else involved?" Shortly after, I was listening to a Christian broadcast where the preacher clearly explained that we have no right to question God about his kids. I believe that was God putting an end to my rant sessions about how and why this could have happened. I knew God was in control and always had been. He may not have caused this to happen, but he allowed it. Both seemed equally hurtful. But I knew in my heart of hearts that God would somehow turn this situation around for his glory. His ways were higher than my ways, and it wasn't up to me to try to figure it out. I had to continue to trust God and believe in him to heal and restore my family.

Another day, while going through the mail, I came across a letter from someone who had heard about the accident and felt compelled to reach out to our family. This person had included an article about a man named Don Piper who had been involved in a terrible car accident. The man had had a near-death experience and described the joy of being in heaven. Upon reading his story, I felt an overwhelming sense of peace and reassurance. I believe that God used this person and Don's story to offer me comfort when I needed it most. I was certain that Angelica was with the Lord, dancing in the heavenlies with his angels. I recalled the first and last dance that Nicolette and Angelica performed together, "After While." As I reflected on the lyrics, I realized that God had chosen that song to bring Nicolette comfort following the aftermath of her sister's death.

The anonymous mailer also suggested that my husband and I visit a local church we had heard about but had never taken the time to go. At that time, my husband had not been in church, and I was attending church alone. God used this as an opportunity for us to fellowship at this place of worship. Shortly after, my husband was baptized as a Christian. I had been praying for years that my husband would come to know Christ as I did. God's timing is always perfect, and God is faithful!

Chapter 13

To be absent in the body is to be present with the Lord. (2 Corinthians 5:8)

y maternal grandmother always said that the dead can see. As a child, that always freaked me out, but Angelica's death changed that for me. Although my daughter has never appeared to me in a dream, I am very much aware of her presence. She has made it known on more than one occasion that she hears and is well aware of what is going on in our lives. I wouldn't be able to share all the signs she has sent me, but I will share a few of the most comforting.

The first Christmas after Angelica had passed, I was setting up our Christmas tree in our living room. I really had no desire to put up the tree, but I reminded myself that I do have two other children who were very much alive and entitled to some much-needed joy.

It must have been around seven or eight o'clock, and Joey was in the bedroom, watching television. As I placed the ornaments on the tree, I began talking out loud to Angelica, telling her how I missed her and that Christmas would not be the same without her. The tears began to flow freely down my cheeks, and I felt myself sinking into a state of depression. As I continued my verbal tale of woe, the light in the ceiling fan began to flicker on and off, on and off, on and off. I called out, "Angelica is that you?" Once again, the light flickered on and off, as if answering affirmatively. I had heard stories that passed-on spirits will go through electrical sources to get the attention of their loved ones, but I had never experienced anything like that before now.

I bellowed for Joey to come witness this for himself. Jokingly, he said, "This better be good," because I had disturbed him in his man cave. I looked up at the light and said, "Angelica, do it again for Daddy." As if on demand, the light flickered on and off. Joey stood staring in disbelief while I called Joseph to come down from upstairs. "Do it for Brother," I said. The light flickered again. There was no doubt that Angelica was there and had made her presence known. The light bulb in that ceiling fan never flickered again, and it was not changed out until a year later!

Another of my favorite signs was the day of my fortieth birthday. I was driving to work early that morning, once again telling Angelica how much I missed her and how my birthday celebration would not be the same without her. I asked her to give me a sign of a butterfly if she was able to hear me. I literally wanted someone to come to me and *personally* hand me a butterfly.

That morning, my students were lined up outside my classroom door, waiting to be let in. One little boy came up to me carrying a large rolled-up piece of oak tag. "Happy birthday, Dr. Nappi," he said, as he handed me his gift and proceeded to walk into the room. I graciously accepted his gift and began to unravel it. Quickly, I saw the outline of a butterfly wing. Once it was completely unrolled, I was able to gaze upon this beautiful, hand-drawn butterfly, a sure-fire sign and birthday present from my daughter. I was convinced that not only can the dead see, they can hear too!

Chapter 14

The Lord is near to the brokenhearted and saves the crushed in spirit. (Psalm 34:18)

Joey was buried in grief. He merely existed and went through the motions of living, but inside I knew he was numb. He would tell me that one day I would come home from work and find him dead. There was no doubt that he was battling severe depression and drowning in grief. I didn't know what to do, other than pray and ask God to heal his broken heart. I reminded him that we had two other children who were looking to us for strength. We couldn't fall apart. We had no choice.

Several nights after Angelica's funeral, I went upstairs to check on Nicolette. Her room was across the hall from Angelica's. Nicolette was sitting on her bed, laughing uncontrollably. I asked her what was so funny, and she continued her hysterics, saying nothing. She pointed to a bottle of Xanax, at which time I realized she had taken some but was unsure as to exactly how many. I immediately called Joey, and we notified poison control.

Thankfully, Nicolette had not overdosed, but she was definitely crying out from emotional pain. She soon began cutting herself as her way of dealing with survivor's guilt. My family was clearly falling apart. Grief had infiltrated every aspect of our lives. We sought professional help as a means to help navigate through the grieving process. Joseph, however, chose denial over acceptance and adamantly refused help of any kind. He was captive to his inner thoughts and emotions and never mentioned his sister Angelica's name. He lived as though he never even had a sister named Angelica.

Chapter 15

And God shall wipe away all tears from their eyes; and there shall be no more death, neither sorrow, nor crying, neither shall there be any more pain: for the former things are passed away. (Revelation 21:4)

The first year after Angelica's death, there wasn't a day that I didn't cry. Every holiday was a trigger, reminding me of the emptiness in our house. The sound of the ice-cream truck coming down the block would reduce me to tears. Angelica would come running down the stairs whenever she heard the music, money in hand.

Some days I would go in her room, lie down on her bed, and bury my face in her pillow. I would inhale as deeply as possible, hoping to breathe in her scent. Oftentimes, I would unpack her overnight bag from the sleepover and carefully caress her belongings. Her eyeglass case, with her petite glasses within, caused my eyes to fill with tears. She looked so studious in those glasses. Inside her wallet was her Christmas money neatly tucked away. She never did make it to the mall that day. Then there was her high school ID with her beautiful smiling face. Angelica would never be returning to Sachem North. She would never graduate, go to the prom, or get married. I felt robbed. Robbed of all those moments that parents live for.

I unzipped her makeup case and observed all the contents within. Her eyeliner, blush, and mascara were evidence of the young lady she had become. Then I saw her shoes, her dancing shoes, the ones she so joyously danced in for the Lord. I was certain that Angelica was rejoicing in the presence of the Lord, but I had missed her so. I wanted her here with me.

Seeing Angelica's school ID reminded me that a visit to her school was in order. I had put off returning her textbooks long enough. I needed to muster up the strength to walk through the doors of Sachem North.

I wanted to remain as low key as possible, as I was not up for the condolences and well wishes. A nauseous feeling came over me as I entered the main entrance of the school. Did Angelica know that she would never return back from winter break? Did she know that Friday would be the last day her feet ever stepped inside that school?

I inconspicuously made my way to the vice principal's office and was greeted by his secretary, who motioned me in. I hesitantly placed Angelica's books in the middle of the conference table. Sorrowfully, his eyes met mine, and I erupted into a fountain of tears. Angelica's lock, which was apparently cut off her locker with wire cutters, was sitting on the table along with the rest of her locker contents. I stared at the lock, choking back the feelings of violation that were rising up within me. I felt violated in the sense that someone had "broken into" my baby's locker without her consent; violated that my daughter's dreams were crushed and destroyed; violated that my baby was suddenly snatched away, and I, her mother, couldn't do a thing to stop it.

Chapter 16

But I do not want you to be ignorant, brethren, concerning those who have fallen asleep, lest you sorrow as others who have no hope. For if we believe that Jesus died and rose again, even so God will bring with Him those who sleep in Jesus. (1 Thessalonians 4:13–14)

*A*ngelica's casket was beautiful, or as beautiful as a casket could be. We decided to keep it closed because she looked thirty years older and puffed up like a quarterback. The four corners of her casket had removable plaques with the picture of a soaring eagle that said, "Going home." We gave one to each godparent and one to Nicolette. The other Joey and I kept and placed by her picture in our living room as a memorial.

The wake was standing room only. The line went out the door and around the corner. Joey and I met and greeted everyone as if it were just an ordinary day. We were in survival mode, doing what any parent waking their child would do.

The show of support for our baby was breathtaking. Floral arrangements lined every wall of the room. Posters and banners, created by the students of Sachem North, were displayed in every bit of available space. Many of Angelica's friends gave their life to the Lord that night. It was a beautiful celebration of life. I knew when all was said and done, Joey and I would collapse under the weight of our emotion.

Chapter 17

But the wisdom that is from above is first pure, then peaceable, gentle, and easy to be intreated, full of mercy and good fruits, without partiality, and without hypocrisy. (James 3:17)

Angelica's English teacher politely squeezed himself through the crowd and handed me the last assignment she had done for his class. "I thought you would like to read this," he said with a grin. That essay became Angelica's eulogy for her service that night. It read,

Everyone has beliefs and morals set in their life. Whether it is the house they live in or what kind of clothes they wear, everyone believes in something.

One of the beliefs that I have is honesty. If you lie to someone they wouldn't be able to trust you again. If you're dishonest with someone, that will affect your relationships in your life. An example of honesty in my life is when I get into trouble and I have to tell my parents the truth about what happened. Sometimes if someone lies, that person will get into more trouble. The better thing to do is to tell the truth so you don't get into even more trouble than what you are in.

Another belief that I have is forgiveness. You should always forgive and forget what people do to you no matter what the situation is or how much it has hurt you. If you say that you forgive someone and then bring it up again, that is not forgiveness. Everyone makes mistakes and no one is perfect. Always give someone a second chance. Give them a chance to make up for what they did.

In your life you should always have a positive attitude. If you say something like, "I'm not going to pass my math test," you are speaking failure over your life. If you have a positive attitude and speak positive things like, "I will pass my math test," then you are speaking positive things over your life.

Confidence is also a very important characteristic that I believe people should have. You should believe in yourself because you can do anything you put your mind to. Set high expectations for yourself so you can strive to achieve them. Don't ever say, "This is too hard" and "I can't do this" because nothing is impossible if you really want it.

I believe in showing people love. When you show people love, it shows you care for them. If you're going through a hard time in life and it seems like every day is getting harder, what you need is a friend who you know will listen to you and have your back through everything that hits your life. You need to know that you are loved and that you're not alone. I feel that a lot of depression and suicide comes from people feeling alone and like no one is there for them. These feelings can be really hard to overcome, so I feel it's our job to make people's lives easier by showing love towards them.

Showing self-respect is also very important. If you have self-love, but not in a conceited way, you will want to protect yourself and make sure that you always do what is best for you. What I have learned is if something or someone is going to harm you, you should stay away because you will get hurt or tempted to do something wrong.

When someone backstabs you or does something behind your back that a friend shouldn't do, I believe that you should still show them kindness. This all goes back to people making mistakes. I feel that you should always show kindness to people because if you were them, you would want someone to show kindness to you.

Another thing that I believe in is obedience. If someone older than you tells you to do something you should do it, no questions asked. The question to ask yourself is "What if I were the parent and my children weren't listening to me, how would I feel?" You're probably going to feel unappreciated and like whatever you do for your kids they don't appreciate.

I also believe in discipline. Discipline is very important especially in kids growing up because your parents love you. That is why they discipline you. If they didn't love you they wouldn't care about how you're brought up and what lies ahead in your future.

Being a good friend would mean that you're loyal to your friends. You should always have their back and be there for them when they need you. If you were going through something in your life, wouldn't you want someone to talk to and be there for you? Well, I believe in doing this for people. Treat others the way you want to be treated.

Everyone has beliefs and my beliefs are important to me because it shows who I am.

Chapter 18

I can do all things through Christ which strengtheneth me. (Phillipians 4:13)

icolette's thirteenth birthday was the second night of the wake. She was her jovial self, but I knew she was crying on the inside. I remember singing "Happy Birthday" to her while Angelica lay in the casket at the funeral home.

We decided to bury Angelica the day after Nicolette's birthday. It was hard enough to hold the wake that same day, let alone bury her that day too.

February 28, 2008, was frigid. Despite being bitter cold, the wind was fierce and furious. I always say that Angelica was pulling a joke on me because she knows how much I hate the cold. Pastor said a quick prayer, and then we all came forward and placed a rose on her casket. I recall looking down into the depth of the grave. The earth was waiting for her body. It wouldn't be long before she was placed in that enormous hole so deep beneath the ground. Piles of dirt would be shoveled on top of her, and she would be down there alone. Alone in that dark, scary abyss. I began counseling myself in my mind: *She's not there, she's not there. That is only her body. She is with the Lord!*

As I looked back at her casket from the limousine, I had an immense desire to throw open the car doors and run over and rescue her. I couldn't leave her there. I felt like I was abandoning her in the middle of nowhere. I felt sick, empty, and alone. When they lowered her casket, part of me was being buried too.

Chapter 19

Be gracious to me, O LORD, for I am in distress; my eye is wasted from grief; my soul and my body also. For my life is spent with sorrow, and my years with sighing; my strength fail because of my iniquity, and my bones waste away. (Psalm 31:9–10)

The night of Angelica's funeral, I walked outside onto our porch and looked up into the night sky. I believe I was looking for Angelica somewhere up above the clouds. I was waiting for her to say, "Mommy, I'm here! Can you see me?" I remember contemplating in my mind, *If I am 38 years old now, and I live another 40 years, then it would be approximately 14,600 days until I see my baby again.* The hopelessness I experienced was so overwhelming, so unfathomable. I never believed that I would live to see another day. I needed God more than ever because I would never make it in my own strength. I needed him to carry me because I was collapsing under the weight of my grief.

There are many ways that my family and I have coped with our grief. We have begun an active mission to change the laws in New York State for drivers who cause death or injury to others while driving with a suspended or revoked license. Also, working in partnership with MADD, we hope to enforce stricter laws where drunk/drugged driving is concerned. Nicolette and I often share our story at schools and other speaking engagements whenever possible.

Each year, my family and I present a memorial scholarship to a graduating senior from Sachem North High School. The scholarship is a way for us to keep Angelica's memory alive while providing financial help to a college-bound student. One of the hardest presentations was Angelica's graduating class of 2012. I have the indelible memory of her classmates walking into the auditorium to "Pomp and Circumstance." As I gazed at the faces of the students seated on the stage, I searched feverishly for that radiant smile. I was convinced that I would see her sitting there, somewhere in the crowd, her petite body positioned in the chair, waiting to be called forward. But my eyes never found hers. She wasn't there. *How could this go on without her? She had every right to be here that night,* I thought. I wondered if her classmates knew how lucky they were to be sitting there at that moment. They were given a privilege that Angelica had been denied. I grew more impassioned to speak on Angelica's behalf that tomorrow is not promised and that life is a gift from God. What you do with your life is your gift to God.

Chapter 20

Judge not, and ye shall not be judged: condemn not, and ye shall not be condemned: forgive, and ye shall be forgiven. (Luke 6:37)

orgiveness is freeing. I had an overwhelming desire to find the man who had killed my daughter. My gift of mercy was tugging at my heartstrings, and I needed this man to know that I forgave him. I knew in my spirit that I wouldn't be able to rest until I reached out to him.

God spoke to my heart and told me to buy him a cross and a chain. I remember battling with my thoughts, saying, "God, are you kidding me? You want me to go out and buy this man a cross and a chain? I don't even have money to do this, and besides, he is an addict! He will sell it for heroin." I couldn't believe what I felt compelled to do, but I knew that obedience was better than sacrifice. I remembered the last time God had spoken to me—the day of the accident—so I knew what I had to do. I told Nicolette to get in the car because we were going shopping.

I decided to go to the local flea market. I knew I would find something at one of the many jewelry kiosks there. I had never bought a cross or a chain for a man before, so I was clueless as to what size, shape, and design.

I walked to the first jewelry booth near the entrance. I looked in the display case but didn't see anything that caught my eye. Across from me was another jewelry booth. I motioned for Nicolette to follow me, and we headed over.

There was a lady behind the counter who asked if I needed assistance. I informed her that I needed to buy a cross and a chain for some guy. She looked at me inquisitively and said, "What guy?" I guess she was expecting me to say my boyfriend or something. Instead, I asked, "Do you really want to know?" ready for her to think I was absolutely certifiable. I mustered up the courage to say, "I am buying it for the man who killed my daughter." I continued to tell her the specifics of the accident when I noticed her face grow very solemn. "Oh, God, please don't tell me you are a relative of his or something," I said, anxiously awaiting her response. "No," she said, "but I am very close friends with his sister." She went into the showcase and pulled out a cross and a chain. "There. This will do. He doesn't wear gold." I looked at Nicolette and broke down in tears. I stepped out in obedience, and God met me right there at that jewelry booth. I got the cross and chain for cost!

Chapter 21

You keep him in perfect peace whose mind is stayed on you because he trusts in you. (Isaiah 26:3)

The day of the arraignment my nerves were a jumbled mess. We were scheduled to appear in court at 9:00 a.m. I told Joey that I did not know how I would react seeing the man who was responsible for our daughter's death. I wrote Bible verses on index cards to read during the car ride. I knew that I needed the peace of Christ more than ever that day.

Three generations of family members swarmed the front of the courthouse. Everyone wore shirts emblazoned with Angelica's beautiful, smiling face. Across the back of the shirt were the words, "Our laws need to be as protective as the arms of an angel." We had already begun our mission to change New

York state law regarding unlicensed driving that results in the death or injury of others.

As everyone began to proceed into the courtroom, I stayed back, inching my way farther and farther away from the courthouse entrance. I stepped behind a nearby bush and crouched, waiting for my daughter's killer to walk by. I heard that he was sitting in a car with his attorney, waiting for our family to go in.

As soon as the coast was clear, he stepped into view. The moment he was within earshot, I stepped out from behind the bush in front of him. I asserted that I needed to see the man who had killed my daughter. Keeping his head down so as not to make eye contact with me, he replied in a monotone, "I am sorry for your loss."

"You are sorry for my loss! Sorry? Is that all that you have to say when you have destroyed my life!" Enraged, it wasn't long before my thoughts made their way out of my mouth, and I began hurling insults at him. My husband and pastor must have heard the commotion or noticed that I went MIA, so it wasn't long before they were both on the scene. Joey put his arms around me and told me to calm down and that God would handle it.

After regaining some composure, we went into the courtroom. I don't know why, but I was the one who felt like the sheep being led to the slaughter.

Chapter 22

See that no one renders evil to anyone, but always pursue what is good both for yourselves and for all. (1 Thessalonians 5:15)

earing the specifics of the accident was like having knives pierce my soul. I was reminded of the trauma that my baby had endured and felt the anger rising up within me. I struggled to control myself from confronting him or spewing out harsh words. I didn't know what was happening to me, but I felt like a cat with its back arched, waiting to pounce. Sobs could be heard from all corners of the room. This room felt like the nightmare room, and I was only feet away from the monster.

When the time had come to present the impact statements, the judge called me forward to take the stand. I slowly made my way to the front of the courtroom, praying that I would be able to gain my composure. I knew I would relive every painful moment, but I was determined to be Angelica's voice. I positioned the microphone, took a deep breath, and began.

"I remember standing in my colleague's classroom approximately three months before the crash. I said, 'Evelyn, I don't know what I would do if something ever happened to one of my kids.' Little did I know that on the afternoon of February 19, 2008, my life would be forever changed.

"I remember the distinct sound of panic in my daughter Nicolette's voice when I answered my cell phone that day. All I could hear was that Angelica's heart rate was low and that they were rushing her to the hospital. It wasn't until the EMT took the phone from my daughter that I realized they had been in an accident. I was advised to get to the hospital quickly because my daughter was critical. I immediately called my oldest sister, Kim, and words of hysteria rushed out of my mouth. I remember screaming, 'My baby can't die. My baby can't die!'

"Upon arriving at Brookhaven Hospital, I was informed that my daughter was in CAT scan and I was unable to see her. The neurologist came out shortly and informed my husband and me that our daughter was brain dead. Those words hit me like a ton of bricks. Brain dead. I couldn't comprehend those words. My honor roll student brain dead! No longer able to think, learn, speak ... I remember feeling detached from my body like everything around me wasn't real and that I was in some sort of dream. To this day, I can't find the words to explain the surge of emotions that welled up inside me because there are none. The doctor told my husband that immediate surgery had to be performed in an attempt to relieve the pressure of her rapidly swelling brain.

"When I saw my daughter in recovery, she was unrecognizable to me, her mother. My gorgeous fourteen-year-old daughter lay lifeless in bed, her eyes, barely open, fixed and dilated. IV tubes were everywhere, and that long, blue tube worked effortlessly to fill her lungs with air. Shards of glass were embedded in her left cheek. Her beautiful, soft skin was all cut up and raw. There was a heap that protruded out from underneath several layers of white gauze that was wrapped around my daughter's head. I thought it was Angelica's beautiful, long hair, neatly wrapped up in a bun and positioned on her head. I was horrified to learn that it was not her hair but her brain, profusely swollen and protruding. It was so horrifying and unbelievable, but it was a tragic reality. I remember these images vividly. I remember the smell of the bloody gauze. I remember the eerie sound of the respirator and the beeping sounds that warned the nurses. They are etched indelibly in my memory, and as hard as I try, they will never escape my mind. I tell you this, Your Honor, because no one knows the horror behind the scenes. No one knows how a family suffers beyond the newspaper headlines. No one knows the ongoing pain that results from a tragedy such as this, from the moment you first find out, to the time when they lower the casket into the ground and the harsh reality begins to set in. That is, of course, unless you're living the nightmare.

"Tuesday through Friday of that dreadful week was spent believing in God for a miracle, as well as accepting the fact that our lives were forever changed. On February 22, 2008, at 3:00 p.m., that blue plastic tube that had been my daughter's life support was removed. Angelica was gone. There would be no more trips to the bus stop each morning. There would never again be the sound of her footsteps coming down the stairs in the morning, or her voice calling me on the phone to tell me that she got a 100 percent on her test. The Sweet 16 she dreamed about will never take place. Her father will never have the chance to walk her down the aisle at her wedding. My daughter will never experience the profound joy of becoming a mother, nor will I be blessed with her children, my grandchildren. Angelica will never have the opportunity to travel to Japan this summer to participate in the student ambassador program for which she was nominated. The list is endless.

"The pain is all consuming. The reality is, my daughter is never coming back. I am forever incomplete, and everything will always be bittersweet because a part of me is missing. The sun will never shine in my horizon the way it did before February 19, 2008. When my daughter died, a piece of me died too. My husband, son, daughter, Angelica's grandparents, aunts, uncles, cousins, and friends feel like a part of them has died as well. It is not unreasonable to say that our entire family is broken and incomplete and nothing can ever make it whole again.

"I would like to use a few verses from Juanita Bynum's song to help express my feelings regarding this tragedy: 'Where do we go from here? How do we continue to live our lives the same? Tell me, how do we try to explain this experience that we had, right here? All I can say is, my life will never be the same.'

"They say the death of a child is the worst thing that a human can experience in their lifetime. I know that even time will never heal this pain that I carry within my heart each and every day. You simply learn to cope. I thank God for the support of family and friends who have been by our side since the beginning and who painstakingly try to ease our grief in every way possible.

"It is my understanding that the toxicology report was inconclusive. However, it is unsettling to me that there were trace amounts of drugs found in his urine. The man responsible for this accident admitted in the police report that he had used heroin just days prior to the accident. In my opinion, any amount, even trace amounts, can impair an individual's ability to drive and operate a motor vehicle. Only God knows the truth of that day. Regardless of the aforementioned, the fact remains that this man should *not* have been driving the day of the accident. He appeared in court that very same morning, just hours before my daughter was killed, and was reminded by the judge not to get behind the wheel of a car. It is my understanding that this man drove himself to court that morning as well. This is frustrating to me. I hold several people accountable for this tragedy: the judge for allowing this man to leave the courtroom that morning, the owner of the vehicle who gave him permission to drive, knowing full well that his right to drive had been taken away, and for the man who drove the jeep, violating his court order not to drive. No matter where the blame is placed, the outcome is still the same. My daughter died. Bad choices resulted in a fatal outcome for an innocent victim.

"Unfortunately, this accident is not an isolated event. There are countless numbers of people driving on our roadways with suspended and revoked licenses. I am *appalled* by our legal system and its extremely lax laws. I believe our laws fail to provide proper consequences to people who violate them. Every week there are reports of unlicensed drivers involved in accidents and causing fatalities, regardless of DUI/DWI influences. My belief is, if you get away with driving without a license, why bother having a license in the first place?

"Since Angelica's death, my family and I have been working diligently to change our laws regarding unlicensed drivers who injure or kill innocent victims. We have received thousands of signatures in support of Article 2440, which would create two new felony crimes for reckless, unlicensed driving that results in an injury or death to another person, whether or not drugs or alcohol are involved. As a tribute to my daughter, I will work efficaciously along with family, friends, and public officials to do all I can to see that this law gets passed. Not only will this help channel our grief, but it will also be a means to secure safer roads and driving conditions for our loved ones.

"To the man who killed my daughter. I do not hate you. I hate that the afternoon of February 19, 2008, destroyed my family, accident or not. I hate peoples' disregard for the law and their selfishness that so often costs innocent people their lives. My daughter, at her young age, always tried to do the right thing. If she didn't, her conscience would nag her. I was told that when she got into the car that day, she immediately put on her seatbelt and explained that she didn't want to die. She also switched seats with the youngest passenger because sitting by the window was unsafe. That was Angelica. She always thought about the consequences of her actions and people's best interests.

"I know that you are sorry about the death of my daughter. You will carry this guilt with you for the rest of your life. That is a heavy cross to bear. The road ahead will not be easy for any of us. I am most grateful for my family and friends and their unconditional love and support. It is my prayer that both families can try to move forward from this day on and begin to heal. Although life will never be the same for any of us, we must press on.

"My hope for you is that you would resume your life after you serve your sentence as a law-abiding citizen. I pray that you remain drug free, make responsible choices, and lead an exemplary life, the way my daughter Angelica did during her brief stay here on this earth. As I stand here this morning of January 7, 2009, I make a promise that Angelica's death will not be in vain but a catalyst for change.

"Family and friends, let us always keep Angelica's memory alive and draw support from each other in the dark days ahead. She would want that, being the child that she was. Angelica's friends, who have joined us here today, thank you for your support of our beloved Angelica. I know she is smiling down on us with that beautiful smile, so grateful that you were a part of her life.

"Angelica Perna Nappi, you are gone but not forgotten. Rest in peace, my beautiful baby. And until we meet again, may you feel our love beneath your wings."

Chapter 23

I said in mine heart, God shall judge the righteous and the wicked: for [there is] a time there for every purpose and for every work. (Ecclesiastes 3:17)

When I turned toward the judge, I noticed that his eyes were welled up with tears. He took both of my hands in his and told me how very, very sorry he was for my devastating loss. I thanked him and, with a sense of relief, made my way back to my seat.

Nicolette would now address the court. I asked God to please strengthen her, as I could only imagine how difficult this would be for her. Holding my breath, I waited for her to begin.

"Thank you, Your Honor, for letting me speak on behalf of my father who is distraught over this situation, and my sister,

Angelica, who is in heaven. There are people in life we can't imagine living without. As a child, I never wondered what it would be like to lose someone that I loved, especially one of my siblings. We were young, innocent, each with a long life and big plans ahead of us—at least that's what we were told. And I, for one, was clueless to the heart-wrenching pain that follows loss, all until February, 19, 2008.

"February 19, 2008, a week before my thirteenth birthday, we were headed to the movies with our friends at 12:18 p.m. A man who was driving without a license went through the red light and struck our car directly where my sister was sitting. I saw the car as we approached the intersection, but I guess I was too shocked to say anything. There is a lot to the story. I remember every second of it. When the car stopped, I turned to the driver who was wiping blood off her lips. She was hit in the mouth when the air bag went off. I called her name in a scared, shaky voice. I smelled the black smoke that surrounded the car. I turned around, remembering that my sister was in the backseat. When I looked back, I saw all four girls with their eyes closed, including my sister. Angelica was hunched over, and at that moment, I was stricken with fear. I grabbed her hand and screamed her name, once, twice, even three times.

"My whole life changed completely that day. Someone who means so much is missing and isn't going to come back because of one man who made a bad choice. Life is full of choices, and it's our responsibility to make the right ones. When this man was told not to drive that unfortunate day by a judge who saw that he had prior convictions, he still decided to take matters into his own hands. He turned that key, basically showing that he didn't care about the law. I know that when I get my license I will abide by the law because driving is a privilege, and apparently, there are some people who take that privilege for granted.

"Due to his poor decision-making, I will never get to experience the joys of having a sister as a grown woman. I will never get to share a dorm with Angelica when I go to college like we had planned. I will never get to see my sister smiling at me as I walk down the aisle at my wedding. I will never hear my children call their aunt Angelica to take them out for the day. I will never have that same companion that I had since the day of February 19th.

"My father believes that the problem with our society is that we can put a robot on Mars but we can't put people behind bars. Our laws fail to protect our people with slap-on-the-wrist consequences. If the consequences for violating the law are too lenient or not enforced, people will continue to do as they wish and show a blatant disregard for the law. This is why my family and I will do everything we can to enforce stricter laws, especially where driving is concerned. Angelica Perna Nappi, we love and miss you."

The sound of handcuffs clicking around his wrist offered some degree of satisfaction. I remember saying, "Thank you, Jesus," breaking the silence in the courtroom.

Due to New York State law, his sentence was a mere 180 days of incarceration. With "good time," or whatever that means in the prison world, he ended up being released 90 days later. The judge explained to me that he had to stay within the restrictions of the law. I believe if the sentencing were up to him, it would have been a much heftier one. My family and I have to endure a lifelong sentence, but he gets a short foray in jail. I was disturbed and more determined than ever to change our laws.

Chapter 24

And when He is come, He will reprove the world concerning sin, and concerning righteousness, and concerning judgment. (John 16:8)

The day after the sentencing, I was sitting at my desk at school when a deep conviction came over me. I began to reflect on my actions from the previous day and how un-Christian-like I had behaved. I never should have hid in the bush like an animal awaiting its prey. I was supposed to be loving, forgiving, and compassionate. Ironically, one of the fruits of the Holy Spirit is self-control. So how do I explain acting like a complete psycho outside the courtroom? Even Jesus reprimanded Peter in his anger when he sliced off the guard's ear. I had to right my wrong and apologize for misrepresenting all that I stand for and believe.

I decided to mail a Bible and a letter of apology to the jail. I asked the man for forgiveness and explained that Angelica was my everything and that he had taken her away from me. I was angry, hurt, and frustrated. The only way I would get any sense of peace from this situation was for him to reform his life and abandon drugs, all out of respect for Angelica. I couldn't get my daughter back, but he had a new lease on life. In my mind, Angelica's death wouldn't be in vain if he stopped using drugs and gave his life to the Lord. I was determined to make some sort of good come from this despicable situation, and he was my main avenue of hope.

Chapter 25

For with God nothing shall be impossible. (Luke 1:37)

here is hope for the addict. My heart breaks for people battling addictions. I am disheartened when people refute, "Once an addict, always an addict." My God can deliver *anyone* from *anything*. He is Jehovah Rapha, our healer. Since Angelica's death, I have become more impassioned to help people who are battling drug and alcohol addictions. I have witnessed firsthand the devastating effects and consequences of drugs and alcohol on a family. Addicts are people just like you and me. The man who was responsible for my daughter's death is a person too, created in the image of God. I don't believe that this man woke up that morning with an intention to kill someone that day. Unfortunately, bad choices can carry bad consequences, and sometimes even fatal ones.

The more lives that are transformed because of Angelica, the better. I am only asking for *one*. If my daughter's death impacts the life of just *one* person, to God be the glory! I know that God is using our testimony to touch the lives of other families who have buried their child, as well as people battling addictions and impulsive behaviors.

As far as the man who killed my daughter, I pray for him every day. I pray that he remembers Angelica and my plea for him to change. Angelica believed that everyone deserves a second chance and to be forgiven. I realize that it is not in my power to change him. Only God can. My job is to plant the seeds of faith and hope and pray that God gives the increase. I trust and believe that God will minister to his heart as well as in the lives of many others he sends my way.

I leave you with a message of hope—hope that you can survive the death of a child. Hope in knowing that God is with you, no matter what devastating circumstances life brings your way. You can overcome anything and everything because God is able! Whether it is drugs, alcohol, or the death of a loved one, you can overcome.

That the trial of your faith, being much more precious than of gold that perisheth, though it be tried with fire, might be found unto praise and honour and glory at the appearing of Jesus Christ. (1 Peter 1:7)

Epilogue

Lo, I am with you always, even unto the end of the world. (Matthew 28:20)

God is faithful. I am a witness. I would not be here had it not been for God's saving grace to carry me in the midst of my storm. God will never bring you to something if he isn't going to bring you through. The Bible says that "weeping may endure for a night, but joy comes in the morning." (Psalm 30:5)

Our morning has come. To God be the glory!

Afterword

And you yourself must be an example to them by doing good works of every kind. (Titus 2:7)

The Nappi family proudly sponsors a Pay It Forward Ministry in memory of Angelica. Please visit our website at www.letluvfindyou.com to share your random act of kindness with us. We look forward to blogging with you.

If you would like to contact Dr. Nappi, please e-mail her at www.atthatmoment1218@gmail.com.

Printed in the United States
By Bookmasters